How to Draw Incredible Sharks

and Other Ocean Giants

BARRON'S

Created and produced by Green Android Ltd

Illustrated by Fiona Gowen

First edition for North America
published in 2016 by
Barron's Educational Series, Inc.

Copyright © Green Android Ltd 2016

Green Android Ltd
49 Beaumont Court
Upper Clapton Road
London, E5 8BG
www.greenandroid.co.uk

All inquiries should be addressed to:
Barron's Educational Series, Inc.
250 Wireless Boulevard
Hauppauge, NY 11788
www.barronseduc.com

ISBN: 978-1-4380-0853-0

Date of Manufacture:
January 2016
Manufactured by:
Toppan Leefung Printing Co., Ltd.,
Shenzhen, China

Printed in China
9 8 7 6 5 4 3 2 1

Contents

Page 32 has an index of everything to draw in this book.

Requiem Sharks

There are 52 species of requiem sharks and all have streamlined, torpedo-shaped bodies. The tiger shark, with its dark stripes and blunt nose, is a fearsome predator.

1 Draw the tiger shark's head, mouth, nose, and first dorsal fin.

2 Continue to draw the body, the second smaller dorsal fin, and the tail (caudal) fin.

3 Sketch the anal and pelvic fins, and finish the body. Now, draw a pectoral fin.

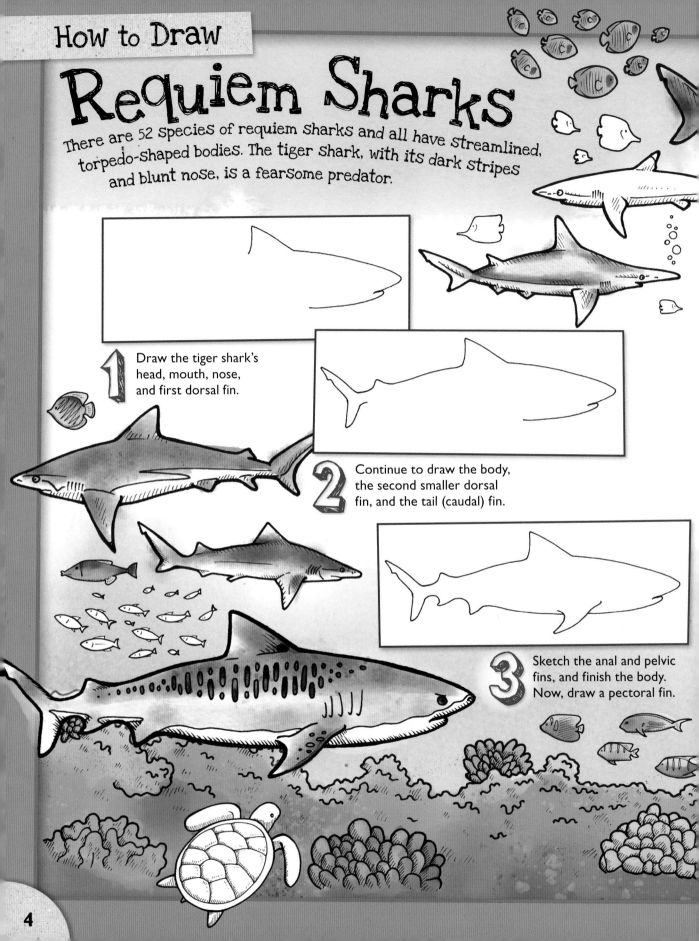

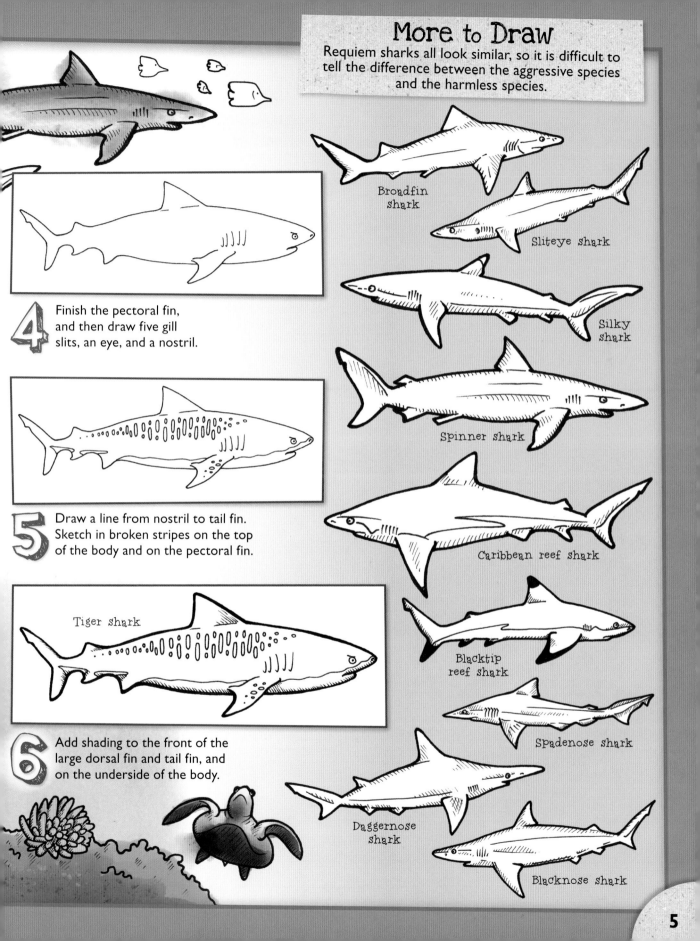

Requiem sharks all look similar, so it is difficult to tell the difference between the aggressive species and the harmless species.

Broadfin shark

Sliteye shark

Silky shark

Spinner shark

Caribbean reef shark

Blacktip reef shark

Spadenose shark

Daggernose shark

Blacknose shark

4 Finish the pectoral fin, and then draw five gill slits, an eye, and a nostril.

5 Draw a line from nostril to tail fin. Sketch in broken stripes on the top of the body and on the pectoral fin.

Tiger shark

6 Add shading to the front of the large dorsal fin and tail fin, and on the underside of the body.

How to Draw

Great White Predator

The elusive Great white Shark, growing up to 20 ft (6 m) long, can chase down its prey at speeds of 15 mi (24 km) per hour. Its streamlined body is gray above, white below.

1 Draw the upper body and fin, and the head, nose, and mouth.

2 Draw the rest of the upper body, small dorsal fin, and tail fin.

3 Sketch more of the body, adding two small fins and a large pectoral fin.

4 Pencil in five gills and draw a large eye over the mouth.

Great white shark

5 Add detail, and draw a line to show where the color changes.

6 Finish the great white shark by adding shading to the body, fins, and tail.

Hammerheads

The oddly-shaped heads of these sharks improves their ability to hunt prey. The cephalofoil (head shape) improves their range of vision — the eyes are at the ends — and makes other sensory organs more effective.

1 Draw the first and second dorsal fins.

2 Add the great hammerhead's long tail fin and anal fin.

3 Next, draw a pelvic fin and a larger pectoral fin.

Hammerheads range in size from 3– 20 ft (1–6 m), but they have extremely small mouths for their size.

Smalleye hammerhead

Carolina hammerhead

Scalloped bonnethead

Bonnethead shark

4 Draw five gill slits near the pectoral fin, the hammer-like head (cephalofoil) and eye.

Scalloped hammerhead

5 Add detail like the lateral line — a line that runs almost the length of the great hammerhead's body.

Whitefin hammerhead

Great hammerhead shark

Winghead shark

Scoophead hammerhead

6 Pencil in shading on all the fins and the cephalofoil and along the underside of the shark's body.

Smooth hammerhead shark

How to Draw
Gentle Giant

The basking shark, at 33 ft (10 m) long, is the world's second largest fish. It swims with its mouth open, filtering the water for the plankton on which it feeds.

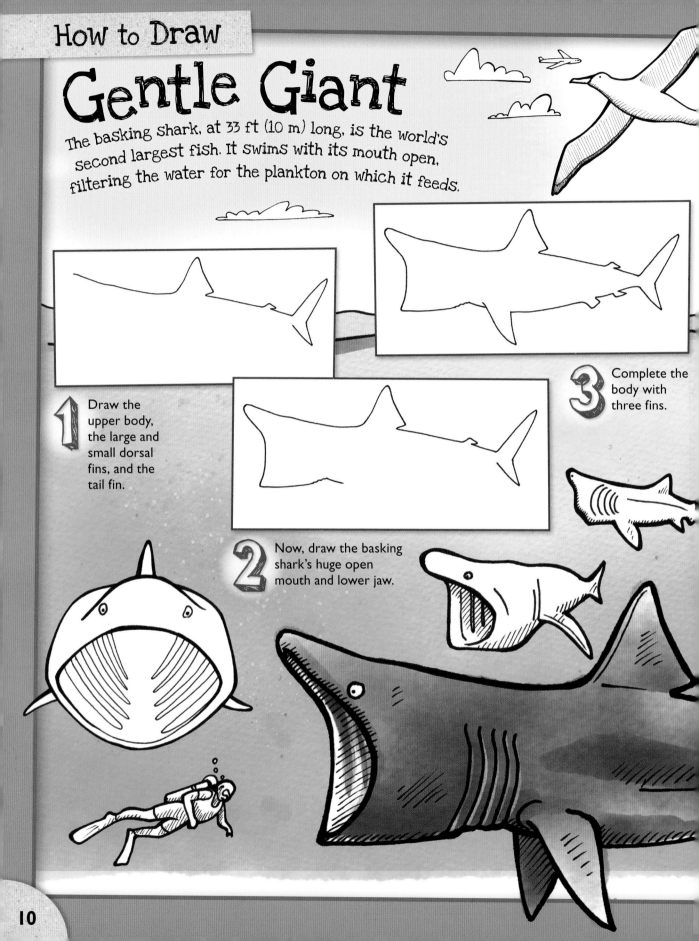

1 Draw the upper body, the large and small dorsal fins, and the tail fin.

2 Now, draw the basking shark's huge open mouth and lower jaw.

3 Complete the body with three fins.

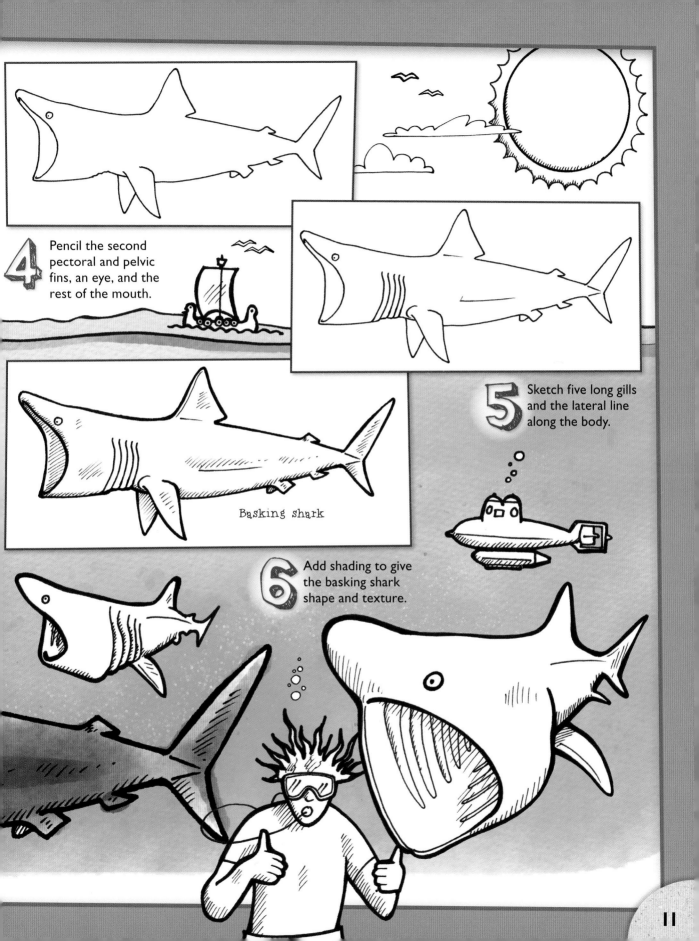

4 Pencil the second pectoral and pelvic fins, an eye, and the rest of the mouth.

Basking shark

5 Sketch five long gills and the lateral line along the body.

6 Add shading to give the basking shark shape and texture.

How to Draw
Angel Sharks

There are 19 species of angel sharks, and they hide their flat, camouflaged body in sand. When prey swim over, they arch upward and snatch it in trap-like jaws.

1 Draw the blunt snout and the start of the body.

2 Draw two fins the same size and a pair of eyes and barbels (whisker-like organs).

3 Add the tail — the lower part is larger than the upper part — and more of the flat body.

4 Sketch in the two pairs of flattened fins. The front pair of fins are larger than the rear.

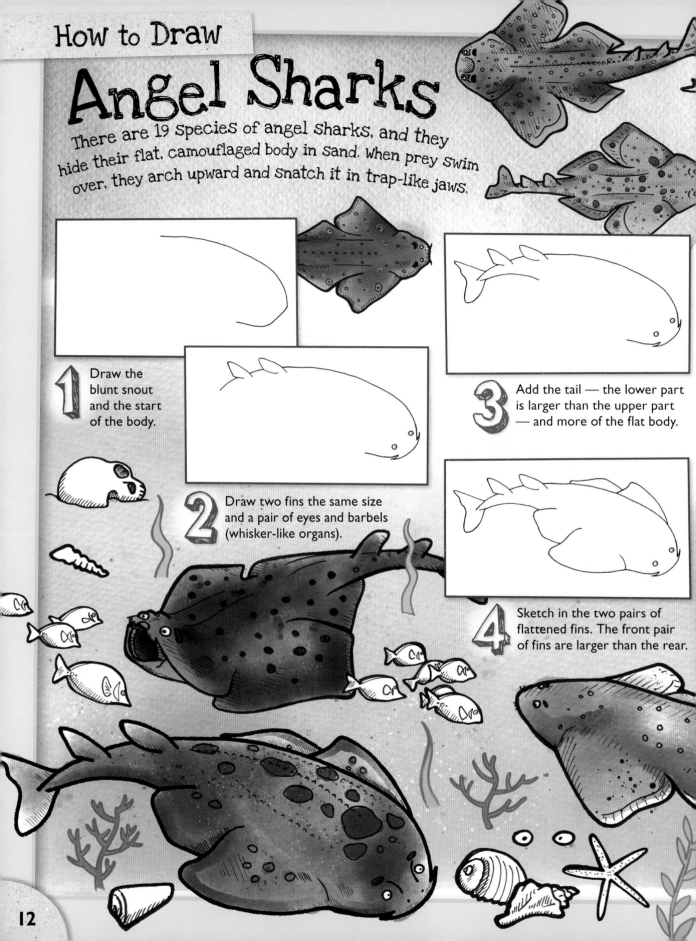

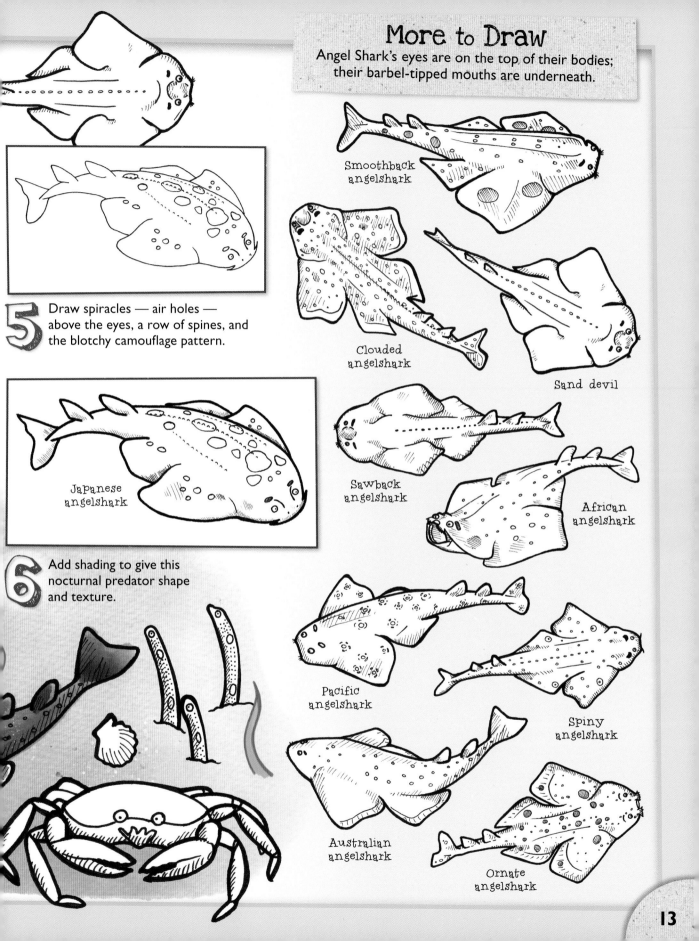

More to Draw
Angel Shark's eyes are on the top of their bodies;
their barbel-tipped mouths are underneath.

5 Draw spiracles — air holes —
above the eyes, a row of spines, and
the blotchy camouflage pattern.

Japanese
angelshark

6 Add shading to give this
nocturnal predator shape
and texture.

Smoothback
angelshark

Clouded
angelshark

Sand devil

Sawback
angelshark

African
angelshark

Pacific
angelshark

Spiny
angelshark

Australian
angelshark

Ornate
angelshark

How to Draw
Toothy Saw Sharks

These well-armed sharks live on the bottom of the ocean where they use their long, blade-like snouts to slash their prey. The mustache-like barbels are sensory organs.

1 Draw the shortnose sawshark's snout and the start of the upper body.

2 Draw two same-sized dorsal fins and the tail fin.

3 Sketch the underbody and the pelvic fin.

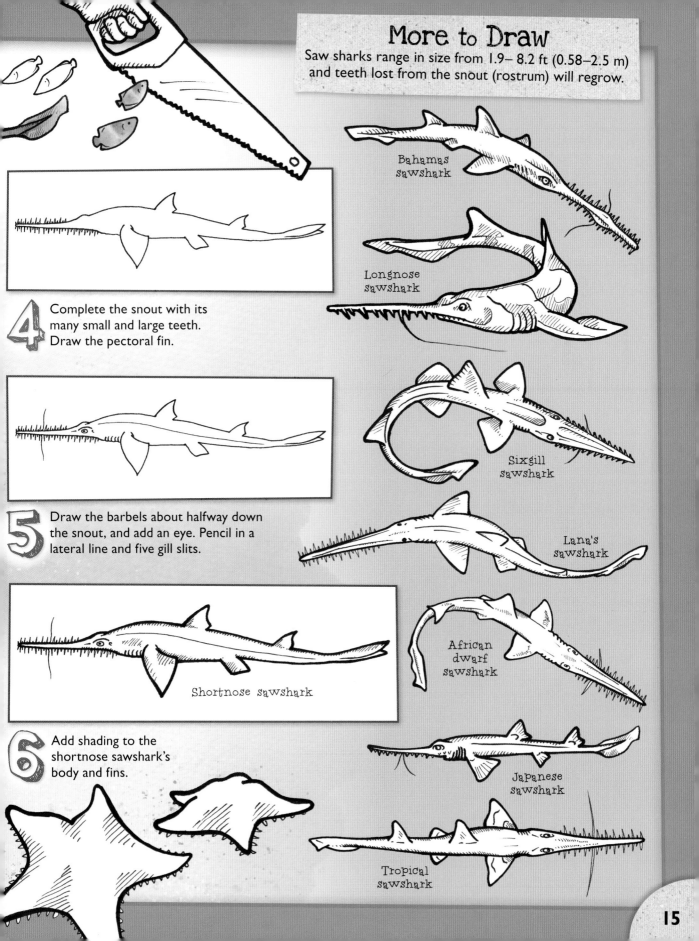

More to Draw

Saw sharks range in size from 1.9– 8.2 ft (0.58–2.5 m) and teeth lost from the snout (rostrum) will regrow.

4 Complete the snout with its many small and large teeth. Draw the pectoral fin.

5 Draw the barbels about halfway down the snout, and add an eye. Pencil in a lateral line and five gill slits.

6 Add shading to the shortnose sawshark's body and fins.

Shortnose sawshark

Bahamas sawshark

Longnose sawshark

Sixgill sawshark

Lana's sawshark

African dwarf sawshark

Japanese sawshark

Tropical sawshark

Houndsharks

There are 40 species of houndsharks, and all have oval eyes and spineless dorsal fins — the fins on the top of the body — of similar size. Houndsharks are regarded as harmless.

1 Draw the Leopard shark's upper body.

2 Draw the rounded snout, large pectoral fin, and the pelvic, anal, and tail fins.

3 Add two similarly sized dorsal fins and the rest of the tail fin

Smooth-hound sharks are members of the houndshark family, and they grow to 5 ft (1.6 m).

Blackspotted smooth-hound

4 Sketch in the shark's large oval eye, nostril, and five gill slits.

Starry smooth-hound

5 Pencil the spots and saddle-like markings.

Whiskery shark

Bigeye houndshark

Grey smooth-hound

Australian grey smooth-hound

Leopard shark

Spotted estuary smooth-hound

6 Add shading to the underbody and fins. Color the markings a dark brown.

Sailback houndshark

School shark

Deepwater sicklefin houndshark

How to Draw

Killer Whale

Also known as the orca, this 33ft (10 m) long, 22,000 lb (10,000 kg) predator is the largest member of the dolphin family. It is intelligent and can communicate with other whales.

1 Draw the snout, head, and tall dorsal fin.

2 Continue drawing the body, then draw the powerful, large flukes (tail fin).

3 Sketch the underbody and the rest of the head.

18

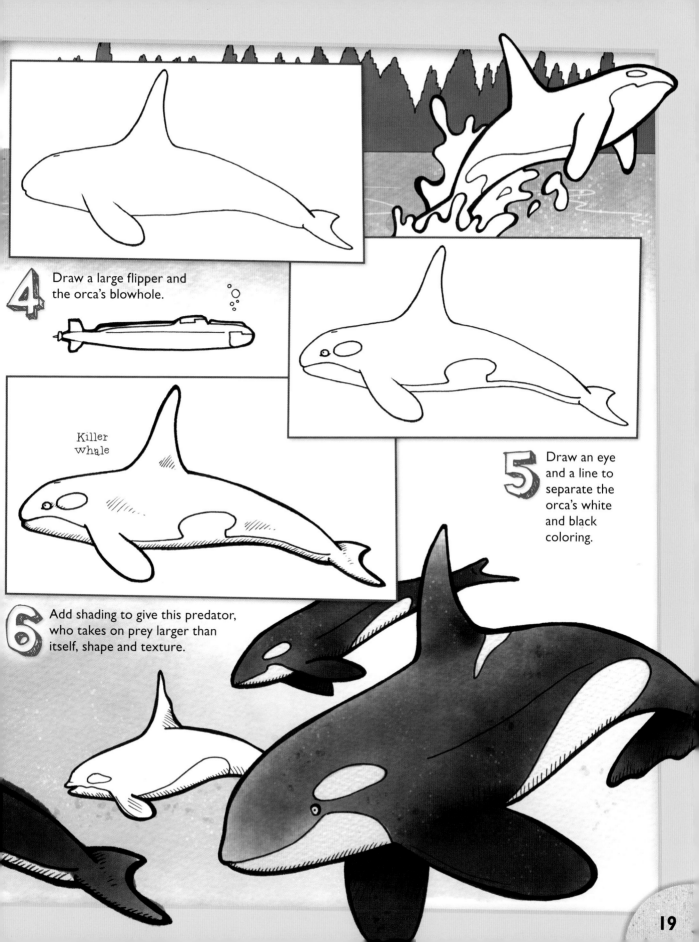

Draw a large flipper and the orca's blowhole.

Killer whale

Draw an eye and a line to separate the orca's white and black coloring.

Add shading to give this predator, who takes on prey larger than itself, shape and texture.

How to Draw
Intelligent Whales

There are two types of whales — toothed whales that feed on fish, squid, and other whales, and baleen whales, like the blue whale, that filter plankton from the water.

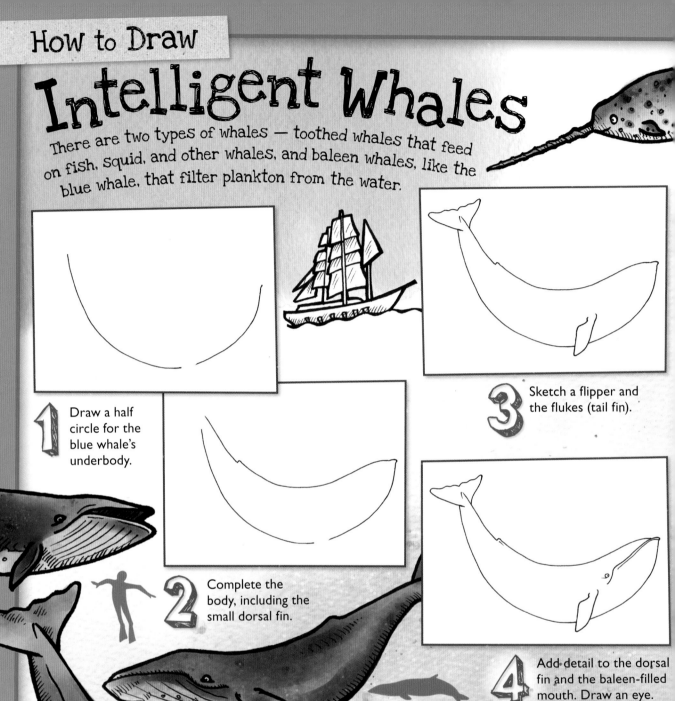

1 Draw a half circle for the blue whale's underbody.

2 Complete the body, including the small dorsal fin.

3 Sketch a flipper and the flukes (tail fin).

4 Add detail to the dorsal fin and the baleen-filled mouth. Draw an eye.

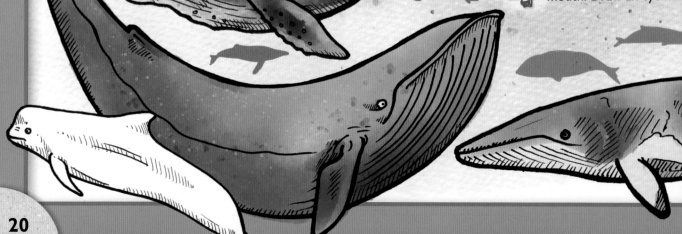

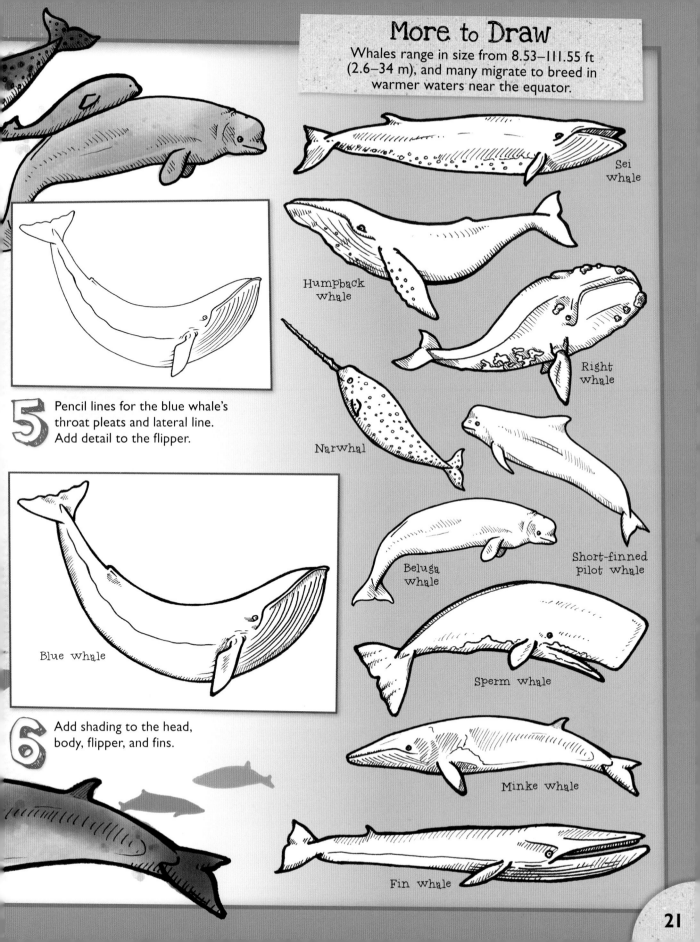

Whales range in size from 8.53–111.55 ft (2.6–34 m), and many migrate to breed in warmer waters near the equator.

Sei whale

Humpback whale

Right whale

Narwhal

Beluga whale

Short-finned pilot whale

Sperm whale

Minke whale

Fin whale

5 Pencil lines for the blue whale's throat pleats and lateral line. Add detail to the flipper.

6 Add shading to the head, body, flipper, and fins.

Blue whale

How to Draw
Giant Squid

Sailors have long told stories of terrifying sea monsters — colossal squid measuring 45 ft (14 m)! Squid have eight arms and two extra long feeding tentacles.

1 Draw two pairs of wriggly lines to form the start of four arms.

2 Draw the head and stabilizing fins. Finish the four arms.

3 Detail the fins and draw a pair of enormous eyes. Fill in sections between the arms.

4 Draw four more arms. Sketch the two feeding tentacles with their club-like ends.

5 Draw suckers on the undersides of the arms. These suckers are 2 in (5 cm) across in real life!

Giant squid

6 Add shading to the squid's arms, head, mantle and fins.

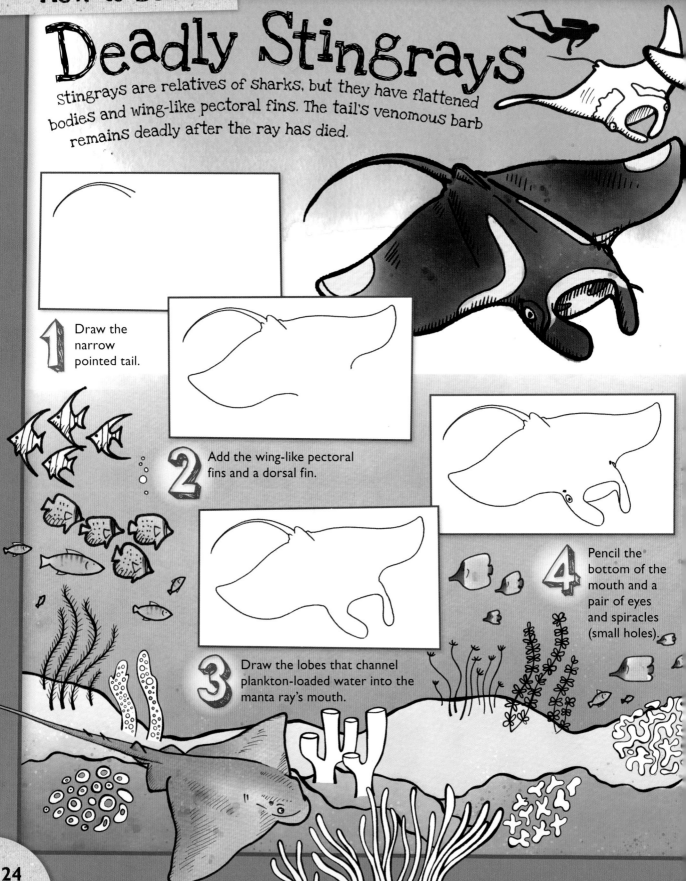

How to Draw

Deadly Stingrays

Stingrays are relatives of sharks, but they have flattened bodies and wing-like pectoral fins. The tail's venomous barb remains deadly after the ray has died.

1 Draw the narrow pointed tail.

2 Add the wing-like pectoral fins and a dorsal fin.

3 Draw the lobes that channel plankton-loaded water into the manta ray's mouth.

4 Pencil the bottom of the mouth and a pair of eyes and spiracles (small holes).

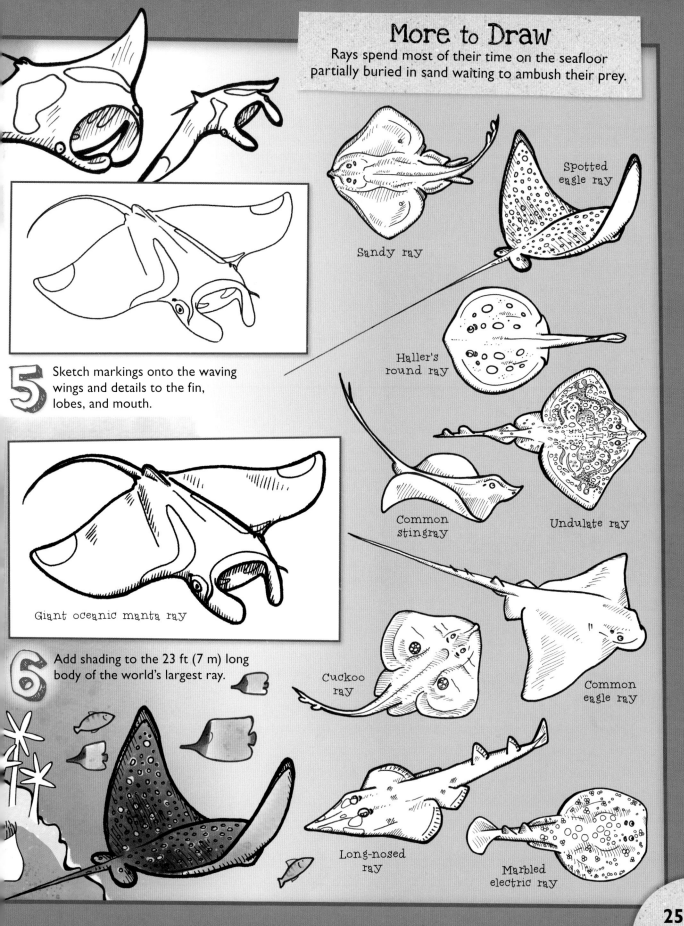

5 Sketch markings onto the waving wings and details to the fin, lobes, and mouth.

Giant oceanic manta ray

6 Add shading to the 23 ft (7 m) long body of the world's largest ray.

Sandy ray

Spotted eagle ray

Haller's round ray

Common stingray

Undulate ray

Cuckoo ray

Common eagle ray

Long-nosed ray

Marbled electric ray

How to Draw
Long-legged Crab

The Japanese spider crab has 10 very long spindly legs — with one pair ending in claws — and measures 12 ft (3.6 m) from leg tip to leg tip. It lives in very deep water.

1 Draw five small oblong shapes to begin the crab's hard carapace (shell).

2 Draw more small oblong shapes and square shapes to create the mouth.

3 Sketch a pair of antennae, eyes, and the rest of the carapace.

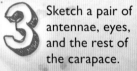

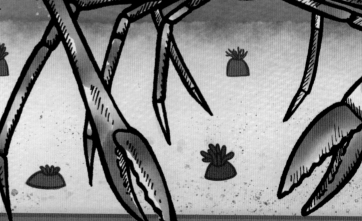

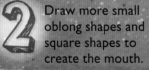

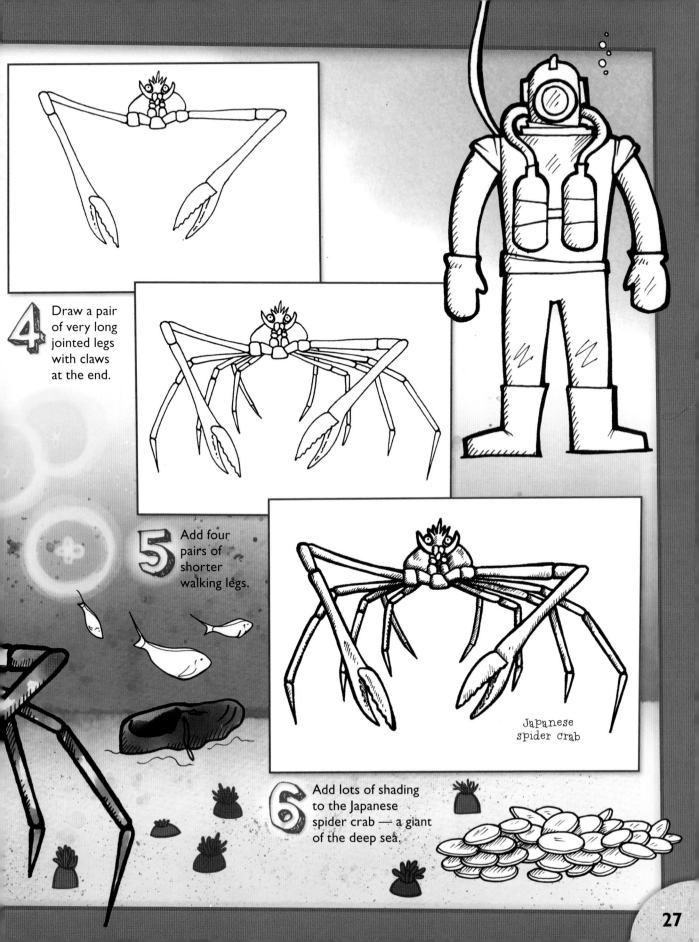

4 Draw a pair of very long jointed legs with claws at the end.

5 Add four pairs of shorter walking legs.

Japanese spider crab

6 Add lots of shading to the Japanese spider crab — a giant of the deep sea.

Fin-footed Seals

These animals divide their time between land and water. From 3-16 ft (1-5 m) long, the largest is the southern elephant seal that can weigh 7,700 lbs (3,500 kg).

1 Draw the belly, the lower part of the body and a flipper.

2 Sketch the webbed hind flippers.

3 Draw the southern elephant seal's back.

4 Pencil the huge, bulbous nose and large, open mouth.

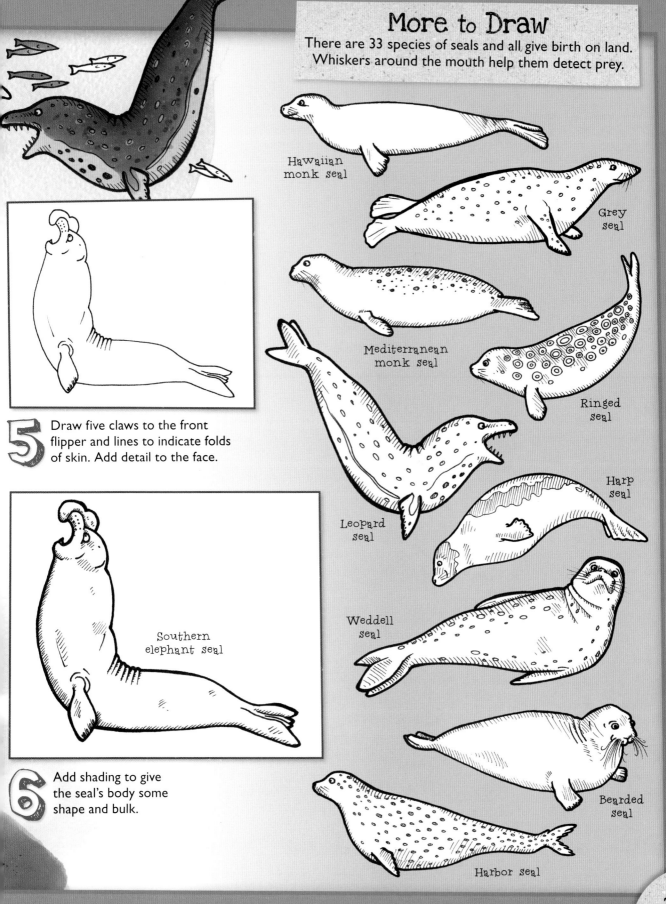

More to Draw
There are 33 species of seals and all give birth on land.
Whiskers around the mouth help them detect prey.

5 Draw five claws to the front flipper and lines to indicate folds of skin. Add detail to the face.

Southern elephant seal

6 Add shading to give the seal's body some shape and bulk.

Hawaiian monk seal

Grey seal

Mediterranean monk seal

Ringed seal

Leopard seal

Harp seal

Weddell seal

Bearded seal

Harbor seal

29

How to Draw

Giant Octopus

The giant Pacific octopus, growing to 30 ft (9 m), changes color and texture to mimic rocks and corals. It uses its razor sharp beak to tear prey — even sharks!

1 Draw the oval-shaped mantle (round-shaped head area).

2 To get started on the first four arms, sketch four wriggly lines.

3 Finish drawing the first four arms.

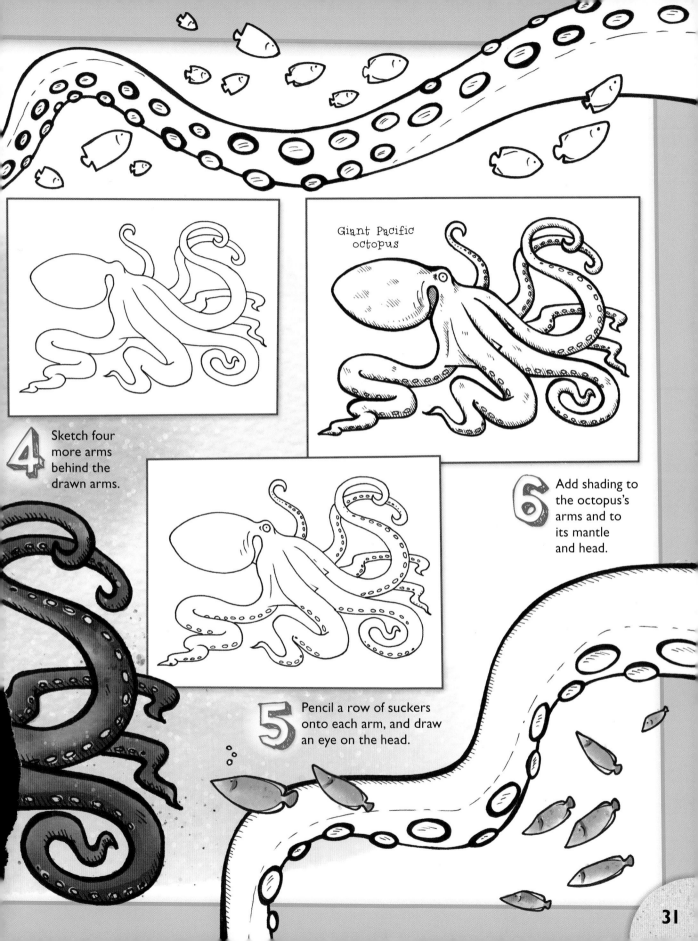

Giant Pacific octopus

4 Sketch four more arms behind the drawn arms.

6 Add shading to the octopus's arms and to its mantle and head.

5 Pencil a row of suckers onto each arm, and draw an eye on the head.

Index

This index is in alphabetical order and it lists all the monsters of the deep that are in this book so that you can easily find your favorites.

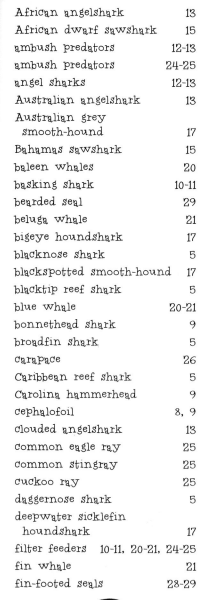